Let's Read!

 Read the Page

 Say It   Sound It   Spell It

 Game

 Repeat

 Stop

Why is wh yellow?

Yellow highlights represent letter teams
that make a single sound or words
with irregular decoding patterns.

The Fix-It Kid

Story by Suzanne Barchers
Illustrated by TRP Toons and Yakovetic Productions

1

Leap got a gift, a big tool kit.

Leap will fix it all,
bit by bit.

 Leap will fix the sink. He will fix the drip.

With his big, big, pin, he will fix the rip.

 Leap will fix the clock. He will make it tick.

Leap will fix the
lock. He will make
it click.

🔖 Leap will fix the lamp. It will soon be lit.

Leap will fix the
ship, with his
fix-it kit.

Can Leap fix a pig?
Can he fix a fish?

Can Leap fix a
swing? Can he fix
a dish?

Leap can fix it all.
Look at what he did.
He fixed it in a zip.
Leap's a fix-it kid!

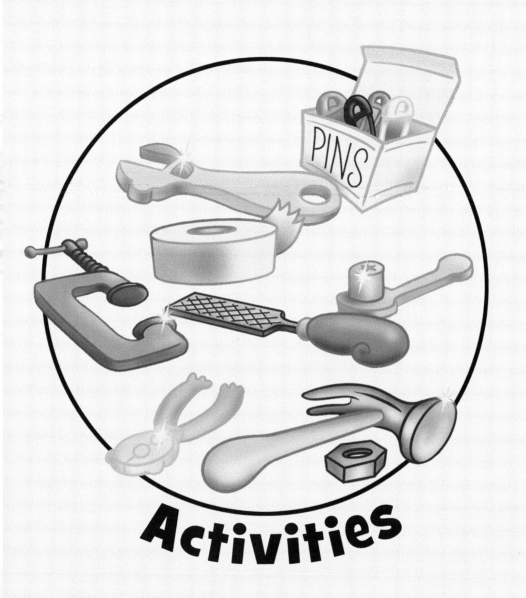

Activities

pig **1**

bed **2**

jet **10**

9

i

e

11

pit **12**

13

14

3

wig **4**

5

hen **8**

7

fed **6**

rim **14**

15

dig **16**

ten tin pin

led pen lid

set bet

sit bit

Words You're Learning
Short Vowels

Short i Words

big	his	kit	rip
bit	in	lit	will
did	it	pig	zip
fix	kid	pin	

Sight Words

all	what
the	with

Challenging Words

click	fixed	sink	tick
drip	gift	soon	tool
fish	ship	swing	